Building Movements

New and Selected Poems

George K. Karos II

Cyberwit.net
HIG 45 Kaushambi Kunj, Kalindipuram
Allahabad - 211011 (U.P.) India
http://www.cyberwit.net
Tel: +(91) 9415091004
E-mail: info@cyberwit.net

Printed at Thomson Press India Limited.

Contents

The Foundry of Trapped Observations

It is impeccable to dispense a trapped observation -
one that transcends time, one that reveals every moment

of progress and practicalities existing as co-concepts
of conviction rewarding passionate ambition

luxuriously transformed by new moons and suns
struggling while awaiting

the recovery of a soldier-
the rehabilitation of a bright drug-addled youth alone in indecision.

Circular Definition

I will live in a circular definition
until I learn to calmly abide
in time's appealing predictability
helping me to abate hate and maledictions
espoused by populist angers
irrefutably forged in public alliance
forever present or abbreviated-
so never to be noticed
in my spherical progression.

Crass Simulation

Focus off me (why am I writing) (who is I?)
as floodgates have opened or closed
Turning me into either wolf or pelican
rising against crass superficiality-
lying low in pompous routines
initiated by spells
absorbed by lurking momentum
dismantling my memory
refined by distant observances
and flower arrangements now dried
by the cruel fate of older paths
leading to newer tombstones,
the naivety of adults
or the efforts of everything elderly.

In the Circles of Progress

In the circles of progress
there exist communities of weakness
silent enough to vanquish
collective blood and namesakes
of markets too beastly for a human price-tag
and too serpentine for demonic reparations
as disparate acts of hope and salvation
continuously promise to repair what has never been broken.

The Wobbling Panda

Patriotism sustained
in midst of long-time wars
of countries foreign to our homeland
where conflicts and slaughter occur
border to border as tempers grow raucous in native soil
allowing lingering feelings of loss and plenty of self-hatred
where slaughters battled within our selves
become waged upon enemies
while foundations steeped in hope
passively rest in the traditional rituals of nostalgia
that varies from persons to persons of dynamic cultural barriers
of exclusive environments misdirected and bench-marked for
generations yet to be born.

I let Someone Be

I let someone be.
I let them.

It is impeccable to dispense a trapped observation -
One that transcends time, one that reveals the moment.

Someone chose to avoid hurting aimlessly and for no reason.
Someone I thought I knew recognized by humanness.

And in the temptation to confront my ego I instead saw their
godliness.
And instead of trying to overpower their id with my promptness
of delivery,

Of my well-cultured stance, of my years of understanding,
wisdom, and hubris.
I let someone be. I let them.

Do You Remember?

Do you remember
The profound grace of the transcendent
A relationship too often denied
Yet allowed and often welcomed?

THE MIND MUST SOMETIMES BE POSSESSED.

Do you remember
When you behaved best
Within the images you perceived
And in the atmospheres observed?

THE HEART MUST SOMETIMES BE LOANED.

Do you remember
When you best represented a personality
Comprehending Spanish moss on Georgia oak trees
Then behaved fittingly as a Southern gentleman?

THE BODY MUST SOMETIMES BE OWNED.

Deluge of Memory Keeps Me Alive

The notion of my birth seeps into my thoughts
Offering me respite from unseasonable moments
That nonetheless comfort my conception of time.
And as daily schedules lead into evenings of possibility
I am continually reminded of people with whom I superficially engage
To support each other's interests, responsibilities, ultimate needs.
And when I speak and use effective vowel-movements,
And as I am ignored, or spoken over (as I so often I am),
My perceptions of other's slightness inform my infinite ignorance.
And when my palpable impermanence struggles
To find firm terrain in my subjective experiences
I renounce ever feeling marginalized, immobilized, or puny.
And when living instinctually bound by objective illusions
In either dispirited publics, or depopulated towns,
Deluge of memory keeps me feeling alive.

After an Election

Things seem so different after an election.
Sometimes political power is offered up
To your enemies and once the power is transferred
Your enemy is no longer just the opponent
But the business partner, the pastor, the diplomatic endeavors.
In other hindsight and perspectives
You either recognize you are defeated
Or that that no one really won.

Diaspora in Channels of Life

Diaspora in channels of life.
I am always concerned how I will survive the day
And the night within the day, and so forth.
Everyone feels differently garnishing empty space.
We are all beautifully alone and aging children,
Pleasure seekers and loyalists to creation.

Circuit Breakers

Circuit breakers protecting this one unremitting space continuum.
Dragged now, or until then, inside one unremitting space continuum
Where children and their parents sometimes create great circumstances.
Humans often wage wars incessantly against their ever-changing families
Or enemies perceived to be worth more alive than dead.
And with temperance, patience, and humble movements
I have optimistically yielded.
I have been taught an elusive sense of tolerance.
I now recognize the circuit breakers protecting my lame excuses
Failing to help me assert forbearance in my association with human rituals
Where fiascos of doubt cyclically determine my anonymity and existence
Ultimately defining my often less reactive than combative stances.

A Disney Dream

In this Disney dream
Responsibility is no longer something
I aspire to understand and implement.
But, rather, responsibility is something of a survivor tool.
Grace from men much wealthier than I.
Much more decided on who they are.
Less concerned about helping others or trying to understand
one's self.

In this Disney dream
Responsibility denies me and rejection finds me
I reasonably and tirelessly observe their adjudication of my sanity
That comes in moments when I perceive their wrongs
And comprehend them, not, perhaps, as people, but as me,
As far as I can perceive, as people can possibly be,
Wrangling with nothingness developing in time and beauty
Arbitrating imaginary reactions to relearning how I once sang.

An Idea of Self

In the drudgery of compliance or care
Remember to stay focused in the moment
For others have illuminated your sense of self.

Cosmic Times

Humans seem like planets circling around my skull
Inspiring hope of respite and allowing for calm to take root in me
As I comprehend, I'm a subjective being experiencing an objective reality.

A Man and a Horse

A man beat the face of his horse with a ragged tree branch.
The man's whipping strokes were fierce and abrupt.
As if he were chipping ice from a car's windshield.
He remained immune to the pain and atrocity he witnessed.

Easy Come, Easy Go.

Furtively we await the expiration of our pleasantries
Consciously referring to past acts of compassion
In mild paralysis yet so very aware
Of every strange power visiting or departing
Our spheres in the ways they do

Gash-Gored Womb

Our home: Welcome!
Welcome to the home at buxom broads,
Redneck guys with facial hair
Inside jacked-up Firebirds
Looking for cheeseburgers and chicks to go!
I can't shower with these boys – I have no pubic hair.
Our home: Welcome!
Laundromats, grocery stores and beer bars,
Cultural centers to our elders –
Parents of real losers drive large cars
Who never miss Mass in fear of Pat, the homo-priest of retribution!
My elbows are bruised by dancing endless pop-culture insurrections.
Our Home: Welcome!
Days of ritualistic pity
Being deemed amorphous, concealed,
Pacified from pondering the relevance of souls
Blossomed in Nile-Euphrates then withered in the pit of
Hiroshima!
I submit to beta blockers but never solutions.
Our home: Welcome!

Window Pains

Today I realized I was growing older
And would never become many of the things I dreamt I would be.
I clutched my penis and looked out my kitchen window
Only to be greeted by a rose bush and swarm of cluttered maple trees.

Affecting a Young but Aging Woman

I knew a young
But aging woman
Very angry with her father
And I believe this affected
Her relationships with others.

I remember one summer night
This young, but aging woman,
Admonished my boyish standards
As I sought modest leverage when dealing her my offer
To buy her vinyl records
For a dollar fifty a piece-

To which she reluctantly agreed-
To this distinctively fragile affair,
As I reassured her twice
With consoling nudge and faint handshake
To respect her guarded treasures
And maintain her melodic keepsakes.

Ode to the Prosperous Comedians

Prosperous are those comedians
Forming lofty bonds
Around sinking stones' muddy ponds
As they parody park birds' chirping
And subordinates' loose face frowns.

Classical Movements between Songs

During the performance
People in the audience
Looked at me as though
I possessed two heads,

One of slight conversation; the other of lame perspectives.

Notwithstanding,
I persuaded my squeamish listeners
To plunge into my comfy loiter
And derive joy from my existence.

Subject to Observer

Actor's eyes caution the cloistered head nods
Of shy women whispering ill-advisement
Into the ears of envisioned standards
Executed by deeds obtained despite crass intentions.

Actresses' eyes drain spoiled planetary powers
Of meek men indulging themselves in the madness of Gods
Who've cheated every lover's attempt to escape gender's
bondage.

Caveat Emptor

(Buyer Beware)

Buyers beware of receipts bound with bullets-
Shot through the arms of commerce seeking targets
Of skin, of hair, of e-mail accounts
Of eyes, of teeth and consumer discounts.

An empire of promotion breeds each dance of satisfaction-
That buys, sells, and trades proletariat's allowance
That lies so brutish, and schemes to scourge
Each interest too conflicted by each labor so endured.

If it were my druthers so as this public rages
I'd forge my humor wisely
To withstand all bitter stages
And remember well dear Death's feeble contempt for all ages.

Regarding John-John

(For John F. Kennedy Jr.)

Squashing your fears
Without Mary or Joseph
By reporting coy thoughts
Of an empty public
That screamed your name madly
As they did with you slain father-
His hatchet-man brothers
And patriots who clamored
Around flag's sweaty bundles-
As wooden pole shook sadly
For each new torch flames' kindling
And those saluted proudly
As they betrayed kindred battles
And stored image, angle and thought
Into half-filled vats of whiskey
Secured from local stock
Used for media's rousing toast
To your new bride's funeral plot
Already bartered, pawned, and sold
By your jealous disciples' rot
Rendered in the exchange
Of fallen grace turned burial at sea.

Western Fools and Eastern Lovers

For every republic poisoned
By factions' steady rise
As scripture bounds the glory
Of aberration's sordid cry,
Shall praises made in obedience
To a soldier's mocking grave
Be inhaled in warm graciousness
With every breath we hold in vain?

For to live among the assembly
Tempting journalistic loves
While wars' debt murders young wise men
On crosses of begotten sons
We must keep our wings clipped
In the childish bliss of point and blame
For young girl hording old secrets
From ripening boys' new shame.

Should we press *stop*
Before *forward*
To press *pause*
Before *play*:
Turning citizen into vandal
And poor privileged into slave
Throwing crack-rocks at the chafing beaks of bald eagles
And firing bullets into high schools' tattered seals?

Has our tilt towards demon witch-hunts
Left our collective pockets

Filled with lint-filled dolt
As alone we seek redemption
In a world of do's and don'ts
As mythical embargoes
Lead to crisis bombing-sessions-
And new brides ingenuously confess
To husband's limp erections-
As we conspire in mass-minds
Where inspiration hides our cover-
Paying homage to slashed tombstones
Of Western fools and Eastern lovers?

Blank Ambition

The existent and inactive
Ignored yet incited with clemency
For discerning between the polar-
Lovemaking or necrophilia,
A baby's cry or morning vomit-
Lessons learned from sappy prose,
Maps' road jargon
Or directions that serve you best.

Universal Standing

The incision of loss
Is vastly becoming
An ornery target
For the man whistling loudly
In drama's dirty puddle
Mating working class wealth
With the peace of knowing
His dead are worth dying for.

Roundness of the Moon

We glance to find elemental design to know.
The roundness of the moon adheres to all we've owned.

We are the mummies whose eyes can never see.
We are the tailors whose threads won't ever meet.
We glance to move uncertain – nasty, hard, shed fate.
Alterations precluding interests - the bold face mask we'll seek
Ransomed and harbored-he rounds of the track-
Hard-earned and fought for-definitions of our past.

Try and listen to everyone talking.
Everyone wants to be heard even when they're not speaking.

Came from a Town

I came from a town
Then moved to a city
Of a reinvented hope
And sustainable visions
Of compliance, revisions,
Of tolerant deeds
And remiss auditions-
Deferring roles
And haughty expressions-
As I remained squarely employed
And often quite infected,
Although employment
Changed with seasons
Of separation from risks
And conclusion's beginning,
Or dissensions arriving
To rescind common grounds
Coming from a town
Then moved to a city.

We, Life Pilgrims

We, life pilgrims,
The various collective
Discoursed in complaint
And victims of friends willing and able
To provide staunch objectives
In attempts to remind ourselves
We are tarnished as catalysts of hope.
We are wayward thinkers too ideal
To be sacrificed at the cost of another.
-

For this would take into consideration
Then demand our-focus to life's rituals of distractions-
And treacherous-minded individuals
Showing a lack of consideration-
For all authority of any condition
Of any wrath or motive
Utilized for personal pleasures.

We, life pilgrims,
In the astonishment of loss
Detained in our search of better revocations
To appease all those longing for power
Where happiness rests in exerting force-
Procuring spiritual nourishment of goodness and reason
Absent of ritual,
Or magic,
Or nature.

In the Streets of the Nation's Capital

In the streets of the Nation's capital
Many seek destination with principled interests
Sharing fragments of useful knowledge
With reimbursements of drugged politic.

In the streets of the Nation's capital
Many discuss their bitter reactions
To parking ticket infractions,
Engagements paid, but rarely praised,
By advocates of communal consumption
Exemplifying a "rascal conscience,"
In the streets of the Nation's capital.
The world's most important city.
Where outside every commercial district
A country road intersects with a U.S. state,
With that of Wyoming's crossing
With that of Columbia's way
Where outside a neighborhood 7-11
Inside a Northwest corridor
Cemented in a sidewalk located due-East
Is inscribed the most ambiguous question:
Who will you screw today?

Morning Today

It is morning today
And destiny means nothing, so far.

Moving actors of high definition
Replace beings of personal interests-
Characters of confused scenery
Cultivate values neglected or left for dead.

It is morning today
And destiny means nothing, so far.

We Dead on Delivery

Forgive us, God of All,
We trapped in church pews
Becoming obedient to humble expressions
Suited for somber states
Of miserable multitudes
Growing wise in the grandeur of commercial hate
Commanding our hardened past
To mingle with the tired and tried lives
Of serf and slave.
We wounded hearted by liberties lies.
We hell-bent inside our master's guise.
We drunken would-be saints seduced by Clergy's Chalice.
Forgive us God of All,
We trapped in church pews.

Sitting Around a Table at Work

Forsaken ornaments left scattered
From a once overlooked country
Have attracted the specter of a youth-like woman
Wearing her hair in a ponytail
Speaking well of her interests,
Winning many minds,
And asking sensible questions
That move conversations ahead of anticipated arrival
As ghostly men reeling beside her precise acumen
Want diligently to please her queries
While maintaining their places
Among branches of burdened reverence-
Taking direction from an appointed guardian of hope-
Listening and interpreting her vowels and syllables
Respectfully knowing, always disfigured,
Purified, speculated, sitting around a table at work.

Frightened of Being Faithful

Fear/wonder/how/why
Earth bound rhythm tides
Distorted by a time of peace
Gather by what others have left, taken,
Less identified, less sublimated
Because we are frightened of being faithful-
More severed by ties to obedience
Keeping life tangible,
More welcomed to attending the only truths
One might ever care to know-
Here/now/today/yesterday
Or whenever someone dies waiting
For authorities owning our wages and expression
With political motives to shelter our mothers
And fathers of ancient sins
From ever knowing less than one could reasonably expect
In the grips of social context-
Forever exploiting dynamic faiths
And extensive lives lasting no years more than needed.

Forgotten Conversations

Sometimes I choose to forget conversations I've had with you.
Usually I can do this whenever you posture within a guise of independence
Directing a rape of my essence long after I've offered you complete courtesy
And listened to you talk realizing your comments have been only meaningful to you
And too scornfully self-involved to allow any involvement of my perspective
Leaving me bored with your own tailored brand of dishonesty
Distorted signals transmitted from your mouth to my ears via voice, or cell phone,
Or any other materialistic accessory you employ
As an extension of your poorly formed self-esteem and splintered personality.

Sometimes I feel as though I'm watching you
From the cavernous depths of your empty soul
I continually try and escape entering your incarceration-
Whenever you make eye contact with my eyes then look away-
Non-verbally defacing our communication with indifference
Reminding me of how my repeated efforts to build communica-
tion with you
Has always encountered belligerent opposition
As you always spoke louder than I spoke
And mutilated our conversations with venal indifference.

Oh, That Game

Rambling, sorted, vengeful folks
Trembling like swine seduced by habit
Pretend to talk with constructed farce
Rearing their heads sulking, dismayed, siphoned
By rosaries of wild hearts once providing for all
What might grow nearer or farther
From abdominal thrusts of merchants
Who never fear sacred texts?

Oh, I've played that game and it helps my mind when I don't win
too much.

I've listened as I've watched them lie
Trashed by civic structure's cups of wine
Fated through chance, design, or luck
Digested by caustic tribes of ancestral binds
Implemented as cultural ties
Bifurcated into death, or time,
Like a prisoner hinged and locked
And utterly confined in public.

Oh, I've played that game and it helps my mind when I don't win
too much.

Getting Out of the Way

Everything passes from portal to portal,
Channel to channel.

Time is on my waysides
Resting its head
Rendering me to praise a modern path
From which I've traveled lost or swayed
Getting out of the way truncated –
No carriages, cars, buses, or shuttles,
No trains, planes, or mulch-colored logo passes.
The promenade is never closed.
There are no terraces, gates, or fees. All are welcomed.

Everything passes from portal to portal,
Channel to channel.

By Half and by Whole

My dream has been interrupted.
As I wake, angelic overtures
Can't be trusted and I balance my beliefs
Like a grown man slipping on a rain-drenched city sidewalk.
Children's voices exclaim
Their indulgent derangements
From a local school's playground
As mid-day's failing light
Beams catatonically through past winter's empty trees
Filled with decaying leaves now resting in empty bird nests
And scaling bark branches that have served
As vehicular transportation for eager squirrels
Focused on survival like a poet creating action
To change incident or plot-
To better the outcome of a tragic situation –
To lighten poorer judgments amidst grotesque circumstances
As Shakespeare wrote of "the slow offense"
And WWII's artists painted "Kilroy was here"
To temper their treasons and lonely relationships
Between knowing the difference between a lie-
And how to function reasonably in a lie-
Complaining to no one or to know one,
Like cursing Tantalus who vainly grasps
For what can never be had, yet diligently pray and pursue-
Continually working to keep safe distances
In cities or towns too small or too close to ever become too near.

You, Them, and Others

A fiancée is dying.
A parking meter is broken.
A record is skipping.
It's no better or worse a day.

Ariel balance is remarkable upon the mountain.
You may never climb the mountain.
The mountain may not exist.
It's no better or worse a day.

You're not sure that what they see is happening.
You're not sure that what they feel is a part of something you
possess.
You're not sure that many nights alone have dissuaded
Your understanding of what you are.
It's not better or worse a day.

Rest is something you haven't had.
You're aware that people are killing each other on this Earth.
Sleep is something restricting to the nature of knowing violence
needs people.
So, you try and relax hoping to fend off the people killing people
So, you might tolerate the voices of violence.

Voices that understand you like finding balance in other people's
motivations.
You don't succeed, you try.
You try and render an inkling of worthy personality.

You try and remember the bewildering reactions of your young nerves
Suspecting you has no arrows of meaning left to shoot through
your heart.

And in the vibrant distribution between your life's privilege and
poverty,
There are communicated new forms of fear and antiquity
Whereby others direct you and want you for their conversations.
They want you for their company.
They want you to succeed for them where others have failed.

They want you to try. They expect you will try.
It's no better or worse a day.

The Removal of Youth

Removal of Youth: Continually disconnected over and again.

Children are laughing and God is everything no one can see.

Removal of youth: Something felt taken away, again.

Shallow exhibitions of denials mask my courage in times of war and job loss.

Removal of youth: Catatonic stasis of exploitation and mediocrity.

Graying hair and bloated belly remind me of pending endings.

Removal of youth: Something felt taken away, again.

Emails replace friends and cash earned then spent on the approval of people.

Removal of Youth: Continually disconnected over and again.

My Vacant Motel

I hear so many slammed doors
In my vacant motel
One would think others are present.

These bursting sounds of non-residents
Reminds me of times in my life
When I was important to someone's decisions-
A friend, a lover, a family member
That longer exist in many nights I have spent alone
Feeling either abandoned or forgotten
And knowing I have died too many times to mention.
I understand completely.
No one lives in this vacant motel but me.

The Year Spent Watching Birds

Listening to birds' chants and songs
Throughout a year where moments
Became days and months,
I pondered three specific questions:
#1. What aspect of a bird's life made them most happy?
#2. What were the less than obvious differences between being
in flight, or not?
#3. What birds had the most awareness?
I felt redeemed watching birds soaring high or low
Revealing what I could never know
Chirping and commuting around me
Flapping wings in ponds or streams
Always cleaning before thirst could be quenched
And flight's destination ever determined.

Who Burned Beatles Records at Public Assemblies?

Who burned Beatles records at public assemblies?

Who ignited freedom's fears and destroyed objective reason?
How long did the flames of ignorance simmer
Into the aroma of people learning to accept
And celebrate their sound and visual differences?

Who burned Beatles records at public assemblies?

Trembling Two

Trembling two: trance or formation –

Bridging goodness with vanity
In-between experiences
Ridden half-way to Hell or to Heaven
And concerned enough to feel,
Remorseful enough to listen,
Shocking enough to neither be properly attended.

Hand Gestures

Mothers and fathers throughout towns and cities
Place their right hand over their heart
And pledge allegiance to on-going sorrows-
Irrelevant conventions that brought over-seas-bombings,
Totalitarian aggression and misguided missions
Where no clear discernment could ever be made
Between sinner or citizen
Between priest or politician
Or predominant legislative body.

Depth of Coordination

Today all is right before me as truth has somewhat changed.
Sparrows fight for chicken bones left littered
In sulfurous stench
As teens talking in jester's tongues
Amend distractions from time allotted-
From a priest disrobing his soiled garments
Inside parishioner's private closet
Or outside a parish's Protestant purge
As Christ's death is sold and bartered
By the allegiance of the religiously convicted
Like a bounced check written to apostolic faith
Never cashed but so often neglected
Like odd pairings of knives, spoons, forks and saucers
Left to be washed in feted sinks
Of blasphemous relations fed doctrine hearts and ego eyes
For every secular sacrament or open-dinner invitation.
Today all is right before me as truth has somewhat changed.

Theatre of Production
Transitional turning typical treatments
Arousing apparent attempts alongside
Constant communities' candid catharsis
Restoring random restless re-assertions-
Bequeathed by badgered bandstands
Vantage valued and virtually vapid.

Spy of Illusion

Looking backwards, or from what once was-
A spy of illusion I was or now am.
A youthful boy still convinced
That long hair and virginity last.

Trips to Europe, Asia, and the Americas,
Coast to coast on planes, or trains
Forming and reforming
Relationships and employments
To help pay bills, gain skills, and become sober and more realistic.

Avoiding selfish desires and disingenuous smiles
After orientations and before all the handshakes
Made me an extraordinary actor
And allowed me undivided attention
Until I grew ill and needed rest.

Remembering Someone Special

I thought of someone special today
I recalled a former lover before she prepared to leave for Africa.
Amid her covert madness,
I had masked a supporting nature
Remembering her willingness to leave
With the distinct honor of my acquaintance.

After 9/11

Tears reflect the shock
of a day's terrorizing moment
where many hours' prior
mourning persons posting pictures
on burned-down city scaffolding
in hopes their loved ones might resurface
from the disfigurements of forefather's sins-
from calamities multiple impairments-
from scores of persons praying
this terrific horror will never be repeated.

Classical Movements between Songs

During the performance,
people in the audience
looked at me as though I
possessed two heads:

one of slight conversation,
the other of lame perspectives.

Notwithstanding,
I persuaded my squeamish listeners
to plunge into my comfy loiter
and derive joy from my existence.

Visiting With Friends in New York City

I spent time visiting with friends in New York City.

As we walked over the Williamsburg Bridge from the Lower
East Side village,

We became very aware of the wind-blown scaffolding disturbed
by the summer night's wind.

We seemed less interested in getting to Brooklyn and more intent
on cleansing our collective conscience from a community we'd
never been a part of, from recognition of the amalgamated
boroughs beneath us, and the creeping, slick-centered fear
absorbed by humans walking beside us.

I spent time visiting with friends in New York City.

When Sarah and I Would Visit the Pigs

I remember when my friend Sarah and I would visit pigs
in the village nearby our home in West Virginia.

I remember whenever we'd reach the area called "Mel's Dwell-
ing" we'd discuss Gertrude Stein's story *Melanctha* and how a
woman named Jane taught Mel "understanding."

I remember how Sarah and I, in route, would walk over every
unstable bridge and try to rock
in aliquot portions.

I remember when we'd reach our sloppy destination Sarah and I
would always try and understand what it might feel like to be a pig.

I remember these considerations to be brief since preceding
conversations regarding pigs distinguished Us as humans pos-
sessing many pig-like traits – like that of languor and disregard.

I remember Sarah thought humans were "uniquely pathetic"
beings that rarely had to experience a pig's "intensely beautiful
focus on survival."

Sarah has grown older, moved to Ireland and become a mother.

I never moved too far away and still visit the pigs from time to time.

My Friend Sadie

(My friend Sadie says people think she's nice and are glad they know her.)

Often,
My friend Sadie
Likes courting neglect
With the same type of solidarity
That ends-up on television screens
And computer monitors of kids
Who drive cars as recklessly as they play video games.

Often,
My friend Sadie
Likes telling the story
Of how her mother taught her
To carry her purse in certain part of the city
Where people pray as solicitously for love
As they sin religiously for power.

So Real Sometimes

Furtively we await the expiration of our pleasantries
Never being able to celebrate patiently
Distracted by obsessions so real sometimes.
Consciously we refer to past acts of compassion
Traumatized, in mild paralysis, damaged,
Yet still aware of every strange new power
Visiting and departing in the ways they do
So real sometimes.

Me and the Special People

Special people seem everywhere
And are becoming illusions that make me feel
My life is unimportant, or of little value,
Or unnecessary, I think, as I now write and you read
And the special people
Direct and lead me
And fight each other,
Ultimately,
And work to diminish those neither angry, nor fighting,
Or breaking deals to acquire sorted dominion or privilege
I suppose,
free of free dating sites
And expensive rejections
I suppose, as special people often encourage
Co-dependence on technology and media,
Breeding narcissism by chance
Or default,
Allowing me to ignore my loneliness
And slaughter my plentiful starvations
So I can text-away politeness and courtesy for good
And construct a country more safe
Than my collective traumas could be counted
And my psychic wars could be mated to mount,
As I'm too old a man to be loved forever,
Too stray a cat to ever have a healthy litter -
Always sliding over floors of empty homes
To emulate being petted and hugged,
As I try to praise whatever I can before I must depart
The Special People I hereby question.

The Illusion of Victimization

I am illusion for the world, for my objective reality and wellbeing.
I am a demolition man right into grace
And beyond the horrible mercy that awaits me.
In any situation I am victim, or incentive for the victimization, it
seems.
So old to be recognizing victimization, with a moralist's tone
tapping
On my computer's keyboard duty bound.

When I Hear Birds Chirping

On occasion, I hear birds chirping
And it sounds eerily similar
To how English-speaking people
Say "Look here, look here".

Not to Be

Not to be overwhelmed each time I change focus.
Not to be scared in moments I remain without being precise.

Opposed to what I would have to consider continually as each
future occurs
In schedules or calendars and waves of time
Turned around either now or later
Before arrivals or departures of conceptions of peace.

Not to be burdened by utterances of beliefs or worry.
Not to be favored by family's trust throughout ragged ages.

Recalling the many civilizations never guaranteed existence
Within the spheres or empty space either moved forward or
reeled backwards
Consuming my navigation throughout dominions felt or imagined.

I See Myself

I see myself. Knowledge of my death is in every waking moment.
The view is positive and all-encompassing.
I see myself. Wanting to be part of any friendly social climate.

All is Remote Connection

All emerges from remote connection
and electrical outlet connecting generations of time and space
with celestial energies from what isn't easily disbursable
to peoples who recognize the difference between ethics from proverbs
bearing our individual egos and objectifications we tolerate
amongst each other.

His Public Address

He approaches every podium with an arrogance that preempts
his immediate declarations of false gratitude.

He will often seem a megalomaniac or smug,
inappropriate. Indefensible.

He will mention God; he will mention family and speak of heroes
without naming one.

He will turn or flex his head in respect to claps of audience approval.

He will quote prominent military generals and classic lines from
successful Hollywood movies.

He will raise his finger and lower his voice when speaking of the
horrors of war.

But he's learned to ignore suffering unless he
must acknowledge or explain it.

He will speak of God to detract from his accusers very aware of
his improprieties and obstructions.

He will lean into his microphone agitated or
eager and holding both hands on the microphone.

He will speak of idle threats – those coming at
him, or perhaps those of others to be aware of.

He will struggle to express regret or maintain
a longwinded humility.

He will be convinced that everything he says is the only thing that
should matter.

He will utter clichés too numerous to be found on any
teleprompter.

He's learned to show appreciation for each despotic assembly
like a clever sociopath scheming.

You are Forever Here, Now, and Always

You are forever here, now and always.
You are the greatest sanctity and expressed in each of my
ephemeral breaths
and in all instances, I've tried to know more about humanity's
multiple meetings.

With your obliging essence, I am equipped to destroy widespread
insincerity
and affirm an adherence to you in both fitting praise and robust
worship.
I endure, undeserving, yet connected to my controlling ignorance.

But too often unabashedly, I have remained grasping for self-
regarding ventures
devoid of your peace and solace. Disgracefully, I have allowed
malevolent behaviors to persist
by those I've known and those I do not seek to know.

By surrendering reliance in you, I obtain respite from harsh
concerns and uncertainties.
Whenever I'm subjected to trepidation and helplessness unde-
serving of your benevolence
you remain steadfast the divinity of my collective existences

Through your most merciful allowance, you grant me existence
to seek refuge in you and ripen faith in your most formidable
sanctification.
During the utmost dire and appalling of life's experiences, in you
I am remain hopeful.

Repeatedly through your mercy, I am reassured of how everywhere
you have provided me with leniency and a potent shield
to combat the bizarre, crude, and incomprehensible.

But like a naively cunning actor, I have habitually avoided your
splendid nature
and greedily sought independent pleasures and the inadequacies
of transient social validations.
Conversely, I have impressed only myself pursuing greedy
indulgences.

I have thoughtlessly refused to accept your most gracious
significance in my carnal life.
I have recurrently acted in my own interests and arrogantly
avoided your benedictions
as I've selfishly endeavored to survive life's harsh weathers by
embracing futility.

Deserting you, I have embarrassingly represented myself.
Without genuine modesty, I have failed to be worthy of your absolution.
Entitled, I've been distracted by the pursuit of prosperity and
earthly prestige.

I have always known you are everything righteous and meaningful.
Unaided, you alone are purposeful being.
You are forever here, now and always.

Flaying into Nonexistence Each Time I Allow Love.

Determined not to settle for anything less
Then the settling sense of direct connection
Aware I've learnt of fitful waves of time
And only visited their breakers during their low tides
Flaying into nonexistence each time I allow love

Dilettante of vision and shrewd master of neglect
I've known myself too well to ever seek contempt
Of those I've perceived more fortunate than I
Or those who've ignored my curt existence
Flaying into nonexistence each time I allow love.

Come to me again and unclutter my view
Regardless of passing predicaments
To restore my human being
And cleans the wounds of negativity
Flaying into nonexistence each time I allow love

Directives of Spirits

Reading my words, you will allow time to render
its perceived sympathetic condolences to you
and that will both alarm and endear your conceptions
of thoughts or understandings.

You'll either be comforted or annoyed by what you read
and compare what's been written to what you've wrote.
You will grow eagerly interested in other interpretive forms
of a verse unlike the ones you now absorb.

It will become especially clear to you that my words
are not simply ramblings but expressions enriched by directives
of spirits -
not of our present worlds but everlasting worlds now astonish-
ingly offered to you.

You will never identify the many authors that inhabit my worded
expression -
images that enthusiastically bend and melt into forms of notions
communicated to you and for you forever, now, or with dates
soon to exist.

You will in due course gain an appreciation and trust
in these instruments of texts inspired by directives of spirits -
that have everlastingly informed substantial and numerous
genealogies
you and I have either lived or never known at all.

Work for it

Wane from fear into forgiveness
Mourning the suffering of those living or dead
As a necessity to attaining peace and obligation
Like plates and dishes broken and damaged much more
Then when purchased and utterly, now, chipped and cracked but
never thrown away.

Work for it.
Address every concern.
With an intention to resolve its hindrance
While working to overcome the uncertainty of the unknown
Like rainwater draining from an abandoned building's the spout
Severed and clogged with the continual debris from many
changing seasons.

Work for it.
Politely resist becoming angry while under distress.
Alerting you of the many alterations of realities that penetrate
your collective worlds
In an attitude of confusion stating that didn't understand your
circumstances
Like a friend who will never lie to you but sometimes throw her
hands in the air
And reminding us of our transience and responsibilities towards
ourselves and others.

Refusal to Wear a Mask

Refusal to wear a mask unmindful of past predicaments.
Shrewd masters of neglect, these crypto fascists appearing everywhere
Willing to protest or elicit harm to any side of a pandemic
On the grounds of state capitals or neighborhood grocery stores
These collective non-conformists asymptomatic and seemingly healthy
Don't like being told what to do and exercise a selfish freedom
So eager to object to executive orders.
What little do they know.
What little do they know not covering their faces in public settings?
What little do they know breathing freely to be infected or
infecting others as they please?

The Sightlessness of God

God is everywhere no one can see.
Time expands our lucid dreams
As progress yields what neither known nor been
Feeding fears' oil to fuel freedoms engine
over bridges navigated through rough terrain
to transport our needs and planned intentions
proclaiming our worth and craved destinations
safely guiding us all now or then again
to empathy shared by sisterhood and man.

We are Taking a Vote

Our families, mine and yours,
Will soon be taking a vote
To confirm our joint existences.
We are seeking proof of both
Past and present futures
Through the act of an election
That will select further leaderships
For us and our anonymously sanctioned.

Stay the Course

No official response on how to protect ourselves from viruses
allowed to limit. Limit lives.
Stay the course.
I will share by love. I will express my love.
I will meet your love I is I is you – I is we.
No time to canonize remorseful words, Empathy spread by tribes
who ridicule impeding failure and strive towards peace.
Stay the course.
I will share my love. I will express my love.
I will meet your love. I is I is you – I is we.

Try Hard to Notice

Try hard to notice.
I'm an old man. With a new plan. Finding truth while unfriending lies.
So optimistic. Seeking mercy – so I try.
Where are our anthems with lyrics of meaning?
Where are the verses habitually sung that protect our homeland
and safeguard our faith?
Conflicts yield self-hatreds that in turn breed long term wars.
Abundant populations protest in unsafe norms.
Codified and rare - the laws that govern time.
Nations fueled by malice destroy generations yet to be born.
The trust that forms in moment's time prevails within our own
mind's eye.
Try hard to notice.